# PETER ALLISS

# MIKE WADE

## THE LAZY GOLFER'S COMPANION

# PETER ALLISS
# THE LAZY GOLFER'S COMPANION

PETER ALLISS AND MIKE WADE

This edition published in 1997 for *Golf World* magazine
by HarperCollins*Publishers*
77-85 Fulham Palace Road
Hammersmith, London W6 8JB

First published in hardback in 1995 by CollinsWillow
an imprint of HarperCollins*Publishers*, London

ISBN 0 583 332781

Printed and bound by
Caledonian International Book Manufacturing Ltd, Glasgow.

Contents

# A TYPICAL WEEKEND FOURBALL

I t is 09.48 on a sunny Saturday; the scene of a typical club fourball, almost anywhere in the world. On the first tee, Doug and Brian have been loitering around for four or five minutes, swishing the odd club and talking *sotto voce* about share prices. With one eye on the clock, as their starting time is 09.50 (where on earth are Matt and Bob?) they are also wondering if they will finish the round in time for a leisurely drink. The ritual session at the nineteenth is indispensable for all.

The 'early birds', an assorted bunch of club members who tee off often at first light (possibly because wives demand they are back in "reasonable" time for shopping, visits or even gardening) are well over the horizon. Moodily they watch the four in front criss-crossing the fairway in the mid-foreground at an agonisingly slow amble.

They turn at the squeak of a trolley behind. Matt puffs up followed closely by Bob, who is struggling into a sleeveless sweater. "Had to stop at the garage," he says. "*Just* in time, as usual."

They toss their balls for partners, the two lying closest together playing together and Bob draws Doug, as he feels he does far too often. They are a well (or ill-) matched pair. Bob habitually slices, while Doug mostly has a horrendous hook (not surprising as you couldn't hammer a nail in with his right hand under grip).

**TOO MANY THOUGHTS CAN FREEZE THE SWING.**

Bob, having the honour, tees up first and squints down the fairway. The four figures in front have now advanced some three hundred yards. "Safe enough to drive off, I suppose?" He looks balefully at the shallow bunker to the right, one hundred and seventy yards out. Nine times out of ten that's where his drives at this hole end up . . . but he ignores it.

Squaring his stance, sucking in his stomach as much as possible, he aligns down the dead centre of the fairway, waggling his driver thoughtfully. Then he freezes for several seconds, swing 'thoughts' jostling in his mind.

*Hover the clubhead behind the ball* (like Greg). *Back low and slow* (like Nick). *Cock the wrists easily* (like Seve). *Coil fully around* (like John Daly). *Drive with the knees* (like Jack). *Finish high* (like Matt – who has been telling him to for the last six weeks).

His resulting swing is not a thing of beauty. It is cumbersome, at best. The ball, powdered by the dust of a small divot, squirts off centre-rightish and rolls across the right hand edge of the bunker. Behind him Doug grunts "Shot". At least the ball missed the bunker.

The others tee off with similarly predictable results. Doug a long way and deep into the left rough; Brian in the right bunker and Matt (who keeps telling them for quite a while after that he's lifting his head) a topped 'worker' centre-right. Happily off without any disasters (as members of the next fourball are approaching the tee) they move after their drives, talking amiably. Another typical weekend fourball ready to enjoy a pleasant round.

But do they have fun? Well of course they enjoy the next four hours or so, after a fashion. Golf is a fulfilling, pleasurable game and around about the sixteenth, with a couple of balls on the match and one pair playing as many indifferent shots as the other, the competition is satisfying. It would be a lot more fun though if all competed better, if all played as well as they thought they were capable of playing.

They could too . . . with just a little thought and a little careful preparation, which is how this book will help you if you are a high-handicapper, whether you're a municipal or a club golfer. It is not written for the absolute beginner, nor for the player who believes that he can emulate Greg, Payne, Nick or Seve. It is written for the golfer who has been playing for a few (or many) years. It won't change your swing dramatically, but it will help you to lessen its most negative effects. It won't necessarily get you pin high out of a bunker, but it will help you get out. Above all, it will help you to play better, and score better which means you should get a lot more fun out of your golf.

Much of our advice may appear to be just common sense. But common sense and clear thought appear to desert the majority of normally intelligent club golfers the minute they head for the course.

Now there are an estimated seven million golfers in Europe, including small active contingents on the fringes in countries like Hungary and Estonia, and some 24 million in the USA. It is hard to compile the many millions who play along the Pacific Rim, largely because a majority of Japanese golfers play their game mainly on driving ranges, but all club players have certain common factors, world-wide. Their average handicap is 20 – and 80 per cent slice.

Many are desk-bound and overweight. They practice little and rarely improve, yet they are very keen supporters of the game. They buy lots of equipment, attend championships, scrutinise golf books, videos and magazines (from which they glean 'tips' which they apply haphazardly for a couple of rounds). They also get invited occasionally, through a friendly sponsoring company, to play in Pro-Ams.

There are Pro-Ams on the day before most tournaments, which give the Tour pro a chance to practice on the course and earn some valuable prize money as well. So Tour pros sum up the abilities of their (usually three) Pro-Am partners fairly quickly. None of them can damage the team's (pro's) score, but if one or two can improve it on a hole where their handicaps count, it's worthwhile. As a result, on the first tee the pros watch 'their' amateurs like hawks. By the fifth or sixth hole they offer a little advice here and there which starts to bring about the odd par where bogey had been the norm.

The pro would have had a few pithy things to say to the members of our fourball after the first 380 yards par four hole. Something diplomatic to Bob (who with 200 yards to go had taken a 3-iron, never having hit one more than 180 yards, and had buried his ball in knee-high rough short on the right) like: "Don't swing your *body* at the ball. Try and hit it with your hands and arms instead." Or to Brian (who had taken two to get out of the bunker) like: "Don't

**CASUAL GOLFERS ARE KEEN SUPPORTERS AT THE GAME.**

try and *lift* the ball off the sand. Take plenty of it." Or to Doug (who had tried a 4-iron out of deep to advance it 25 yards) like: "Next time use your *wedge* and aim for the nearest bit of fairway."

With Matt he would be reserving judgment because after another skinny one, Matt had pitched to the fringe and fired a putt that rocketed in off the pin. His fluky par won the hole over two bogeys and a double. They had all left the green happily. Things would certainly improve once they got into their game.

How different it could all have been. Bob's dream when he stood on the first tee (sorry to be picking on him but he's a good example of a typical club player), was to crack a drive quail-high 250 yards down the middle. The reality we know, but with a little common sense he could have played the hole much better, while *making the best* of what he had in terms of swing and ability.

First, arriving "just in time" without a chance to loosen up virtually guarantees a cranky shot. That is not to say you should spend half an hour on the practice ground before every round: in the time-stressed 1990s few have time to spare and club golfers mostly hate practising. And indeed, how many golf clubs in the UK have decent practice facilities of any sort? But virtually everyone has played tennis at some time. Would you consider going straight onto a court and with your first movement hit a serve in the first 'scoring' game, even if it's a friendly match? Of course not. You'd have a short knock-up first – and that is what club golfers should do, even if it's a few putts on the putting green and a couple of chips.

Second, Bob did not use the grey matter between his ears which constitutes a large part of the simple game of golf. He had been in a bunker at the first nine times out of ten, yet he still aimed *straight* down the fairway. Knowing he always sliced, he should have teed up on the right hand side of the tee and aimed at the left hand rough where Doug ended up. With his usual swing, he would probably have ended up in the middle of the fairway and very likely have hit the ball twenty yards or so further.

Third, no one can swing fluidly, if they have umpteen swing thoughts jostling in their minds. You can never get a natural-looking, effective, repeating swing that way. At the most, you can hold *one* swing thought for the day ("Swing *slower*" is often a good one).

Fourth, Bob's second shot to the green was a combination of nonsense and vanity. Once you've got off the tee, it's the *second* shot that make the difference in scoring for the player. Underclubbing is the major fault (as it often is on long par three holes).

Finally (although there are many other lessons to be learned from this role model performance) Bob took his driver off the first tee. Now it's all very well hitting your *drive* at the start if you've hit quite a few on the practice ground before the game. But in Bob's case, driving off with the most difficult club in his bag did not make sense. Added to which his driver had a swing weight and lie designed for a six foot four, athletic 20-year-old, which Bob certainly is not!

And that brings us to one of the most important factors for the club golfer, the 'tools of the trade' – your golf clubs.

# REMEDIES FOR SLICE AND HOOK

A dictionary definition of the word 'affliction' is "a state or cause of grievous distress." That definition, for the great majority of club players could equally be applied to the word 'slice'. For more than 80 per cent of all golfers are habitual slicers – and barely one in 50 knows the reason why. It is extraordinary how reasonably intelligent, healthy, well co-ordinated people can be so afflicted. It would seem that slicing is endemic to golf courses and driving ranges worldwide. Little wonder that so many are forever searching for a cure, any cure, that will alleviate their suffering.

*The bad news* is that there is no panacea. The reason why a ball slices is because the club face is open to the swing line at impact.

The club face stays open for a myriad of reasons. It's all down to the swing line and the approach of the club as it comes into the ball. The set-up plays a big part, the ball position equally so, and then how you move your body throughout the swing also has a very major impact as to where the ball goes.

*The good news* – is that, while all swings are individual, depending on height, build and age, slicers fall into certain clear categories. If you slice, you're a *ball forward player* or a *body action spinner*, an *upright tilter* or a *reverse pivoter*. You could equally be a *spine jerker*, a *weak swinger*, or a *shoulder shover*. All these are different categories of a slicer and if you have been trying a cure, gleaned from magazines, instruction books or TV, and it hasn't worked, it could be that you've been taking the wrong medicine, trying a cure for a different category to the one you're in.

So let's review the symptoms of the different sufferers, with a suggested treatment for each one. If you can diagnose just how you slice from these examples (and also seek the 'specialist opinion' of your club pro, as you should) then you could alleviate your pernicious slice, forever.

A SLICE COMING UP.

## The Wrong Place at the Wrong Time

Just why so many golfers play the ball too far forward in their stance and subsequently slice is hard to determine. It probably comes from their first few rounds as a beginner, when they did not understand the importance of getting their set-up correct, their line-up correct and the ball in the right hittable position. Most people don't stand square to the ball because they feel they're in their own way, so the natural thing for 99 per cent of people who take up golf is to aim left with the ball forward and try and sort of push it away. They have no idea of taking a back swing. People who have played hockey or cricket have some idea of lifting a stick, bat or club to give a ball a whack and that's why most of them make a pretty good fist at golf if they give it a bit of time and effort.

Hitting with the shoulders is also infectious. Golfers have often heard their peers say of a particularly long drive that the striker had "really opened his shoulders on that one". It is a meaningless term, for open shoulders at address can certainly cause a slice, as does hitting with them. In such a case, a player can set up well, with a good grip and make a fluid backswing. At the top, possibly because he freezes, tries to use his shoulders for distance, or locks his swing with a stiff right knee, he starts his downswing with his shoulders. His right one rolls round instead of under, throwing his swing from out to in and his hands are carried through the ball way ahead of the clubhead. Yet another slice results.

The more he slices the more he aims to the left. The more he aims to the left the more he comes across the ball and the more he slices. You can ally that to table tennis or tennis. When you're driving a ball over the net or on a table tennis table, extend your right hand as if you're going to smack somebody across the face and then you take it back. As you hit the ball, the hand rolls over and the palm goes down towards the surface of the table or the ground, which creates a flat shot with a little bit of draw. If you want to slice it, cut it, chop it, the opposite occurs. You take the racket out and across the ball slicing across imparting side spin. That's pretty well the characteristics which are very similar to hooking and slicing at golf and the way the clubhead comes into the ball. If you want to stop slicing (and John Jacobs, the great teacher, once had a proud boast that he could stop anybody slicing within a maximum of a dozen golf balls, perhaps half that number) take a 2-wood, adjust your stance, get the ball in a different position and swing from the inside and then round. Slicing is usually the result of a wood chopping action.

Bob, the stalwart member of our fourball, is a classic example of this category of *ball forward player*. Watch him on the tee. In aiming to the left (which he also does because he has a fuller figure and can thereby see the flag a little more easily) he sets the ball too far forward in his stance. This, with his openly aligned shoulders, effectively weakens his grip. His right hand sits well on top of his left, which has half a knuckle showing, and his arms are stretched out and rigid. His right shoulder is too high as well.

As a result, when Bob starts his takeaway, he has to fight taking the club straight back. So he pulls his arms inside on too flat a plane, rolling the club face open. At the top his body recoil shoves his right shoulder out, throwing his arms in a steep out to in swingpath. Coupled with his weakened grip, the ball flies off left before curling right, although maddeningly the odd one keeps on going straight left, as do his short irons.

At least, given this shot pattern, Bob can manage to play a round breaking 100, scoring less if he aims left with his longer clubs instead of stubbornly pointing down the middle. But how much better it would be if he hit through the ball with the club face square to the target when he was aligned square to it himself. To achieve this there is a simple cure – although knowing it and applying it are two different things. All Bob has to do is to understand *why* he is slicing. Then he has to set the ball further back in his stance (three inches inside his left heel) when his club face, shoulders and feet are square to the target line. This will have the effect of naturally strengthening his grip. Finally, he has to get out of the habit of rolling, or fanning, his club on the takeaway and swing back without manipulating it with his hands.

You too have to take this medicine if you're a ball forward player – and it can be very difficult to swallow. When you are correctly lined up to swing your club back on an inside path and then down along the target line, you will probably feel decidedly uncomfortable (particularly if you've sliced most of your golfing life). It will seem

**WHEN THE BALL IS TOO FAR FORWARD, THE RIGHT SHOULDER MOVES OUT AND OVER.**

that you are about to compound your slice by hitting the ball out to the right. Yet you have to find out that you can swing from the inside out to the right to hit the ball straight. So head for the practice ground (just for once) and set up square. Before you hit any balls, place a club between your feet and the ball position, angled a few degrees right of your target line. If you swing back parallel with its shaft, you'll be on a natural inside path. Forget your anxiety. Just keep your eye on the back of the ball, swing back along the shaft line and . . . watch the result.

There's another drill you can try out to help you swing back correctly, although it's quite difficult to control at first, so watch out for anyone standing nearby. Simply hit some balls using your right arm only, teed up off your right heel. Use your 8-iron and set up square. You will find that your right shoulder will be lower at address and you will swing from inside to along the target line. It can pay dividends in ironing out that left to right flight.

The *body action spinner* also needs advice to cure the same distressing shot pattern. To diagnose his condition, he should note that while he mostly slices, some of his shots are skied high, while the occasional one dribbles along the fairway to the left.

There's nothing usually wrong with his ball position, set-up, takeaway or backswing. The trouble comes in the downswing – and what causes the complaint is probably all in the mind. Maybe he tries too hard to 'start the downswing with a turn of the left hip'. Or perhaps, particularly if he is a senior golfer, he strives for the 'late hit' position so encouraged in the teaching of the 1950s and '60s. Or he could have been admonished before, having dug several deep divots, that he was 'casting his hands from the top'.

Whatever the primary cause, his downswing is bodged. Sliding and spinning his hips too soon, he seems to be trying to hit the ball with his body, as his arms swing down too late. If he grips too tightly to stop casting, he also locks his hands and arms which, given his excessive body spin, throws his right shoulder out and the club comes down on a steep out to in path.

If you are in this category of slicer you will have to learn to stop swinging yourself instead of the club. The specific is to practice swinging with legs and feet touching. Tee up the ball, use a five or six iron and simply swing the club up and down with the arms. You will have to anyway. If you try and force the swing with conscious hip or leg action, or power it with your shoulders, you will immediately lose your balance. You won't be able to swing too fast either.

If you find that you are throttling the club involuntarily, and not getting enough swish as you hit the ball, make a series of half swings with the hands apart on the grip. You'll see the club flash through the hitting area and condition yourself to a free release of the hands. You should not be surprised when you start striking the ball squarely, sending it soaring straight on line (if it doesn't, check your alignment). But you will be surprised at the distance you get from the feet together swing. It will only be some ten yards shorter than your best efforts from your normal swing. Hopefully, when you've applied the specific, your best efforts will become your norm.

## The Reverse Pivot

The *upright tilter* is another category of slicer which is common among club golfers. Now rocking and tilting the right shoulder upwards on the backswing, rather than letting it turn away naturally, is a fault that can also develop in the swings of a number of good golfers, including probably the greatest of all time, Jack Nicklaus. He has spoken and written openly about his affliction, which he took positive steps to cure in 1980.

Jack always strived for a long, high flying shot, which demanded a big, high swing arc. But in his early days his very upright swing was also 'deep' (the club at the top being above or even behind his right shoulder) for he had a very strong coil. Then his backswing gradually changed for a number of reasons, possibly through playing in windier conditions in Florida. It stayed steep, but lost its depth. He didn't coil fully, for the more directly upwards the arms swing, the sooner the body stops coiling. Also the more upright the swing, the steeper the downswing and the harder it is to hit the ball squarely.

As a result, Jack suffered from a feeling of hitting the ball badly, obliquely, and he lost distance. But with his considerable ability and experience, he could still control the ball sufficiently despite the affliction. He could still think his way around a golf course, he could certainly still putt and he could still win. This is not the case for the average golfer who is an upright tilter; mostly all he can do is slice.

Matt, the tallest, youngest member of our fourball, is a prime example. Most of his long shots start off straightish before swinging right and he often thins shots, although he occasionally hits one fat. The root cause of this is bad posture. Matt sets up with his back and neck bent too far forwards over the ball, possibly determined to 'keep his head down'. Now the more inclined he is at address, the more his shoulders (and hips) will rock and tilt upwards, rather than turn, on the backswing. This, subsequently, causes a slide and blocks the body coming down. The left side doesn't clear and this forces the club into a steep downwards arc in which the hands and arms can't square the club face in time.

Jack Nicklaus' cure would also work for Matt. First, Jack started to stand much taller to the ball, setting up with his back more upright and his head up. When he began to address the ball in this way, he said that he felt uncomfortable (like, he imagined, many golfers who slice feel most of the time). But this taller posture allowed his right shoulder to turn properly and his body to clear as he swung through.

Another element in his cure (which might not be applicable to all upright tilters) was to set up with his head more in the centre of his stance. Previously he used to address the ball with his head 'back', much nearer his right side, to ensure against it being pulled forwards by his strong leg drive. His more centred head made it easier for him to swing back on an inside path, as did the final element of his cure, letting his right elbow fold earlier on the backswing. If you are an upright tilter, you might try the same prescription; if it worked for Jack, it could work for you.

Over-upright, uncoiled swings are also the symptoms of another category of slicer: the *reverse pivoter*. Here the sufferer finds himself leaning to the left at the top and he then falls back onto his right foot as he swings down, losing distance and often slicing severely. Diagnosing the affliction is easy; you'll find yourself leaning left at the top, then as you 'fire and fall back' your right foot will be flat on the ground. But the causes of this are several, as are the cures, which concern the set-up (again) of hands, arms and head.

First, and perhaps rather obviously (though not to him) is the golfer who sets up with much of his weight on his left side. He may well not do this deliberately: it can stem from a strong grip with the hands several inches ahead of the ball. From that position, he can only swing the club straight back, with little turn as the weight stays left, which forces his weight right coming down. The cure is easy. He should check his set-up and ensure that he's evenly balanced, with his hands just ahead of (or hovering over) the ball.

Over active hands though can cause a reverse pivot, even if your set-up is OK. When hands are too active in the takeaway they can push the clubhead way outside the target line, which means that you swing too steeply. To cure this variation, firm up your grip to quiet your hand action and concentrate on swinging your arms away. Check that when the shaft of the club is parallel to the ground it is also parallel to the target line. That way you'll be on plane for a good shot.

Arms, particularly the left one, can also lead to the reverse pivot. They should certainly not be too rigid as you set up: they should dangle in a firm, yet relaxed way. However if your left arm gets too relaxed and if you let it *bend* too much on the backswing, you'll be too upright, won't coil properly and will reverse pivot. The cure is to swing back the left arm as straight as you can without straining, deliberately trying to swing flatter, until your weight shifts naturally right at the top. When it does that, it will move automatically left coming down.

Finally, for certain reverse pivoters, it all comes to the head. Practically every golfer has been told firmly at some time to keep his head still. Some have also been instructed not to sway as they swing (despite the example of Curtis Strange, whose different, yet effective technique won him two US Opens). However, while coiling, not swaying, around a steady spine and head is fundamental to good golf, some golfers carry the still head position to an extreme.

Rigidly holding their heads immobile, they tense up their bodies and their arms and swing back into . . . a reverse pivot. The prescription? Forget about the head. Let it move slightly to the right going back if it wants to. Just concentrate on swinging smoothly and the head will take care of itself.

## Spine Jerkers and Others

Posture is clearly very important for good golf. A top pro always looks balanced over the ball, leaning forward from his hips, knees flexed, arms extended, with his back (and spine) at an angle of some 30 degrees to the vertical. Moreover, during his swing through impact, this angle of inclination does not change. This is not the case with many golfers, who are afflicted with a jerky movement in the downswing, dipping or lifting their spines, which can cause an out to in swing and a slice.

If you are such a *spine jerker*, bad posture is the prime cause – and there is also a good chance that you're a little shorter than average height, or on the other hand a lot taller. The shorter golfer can get into bad habits by bending his knees too much at address. He sets up with too upright a spine angle (say 15 degrees) his feet spread wide and his weight back on his heels. As his weight shifts naturally further backwards at the top, he tends to jerk forward on the downswing, dipping his spine and scything out to in. His cure is to get his posture right from the start. He must bend more from the hips, with less flex in his knees, a narrower stance and his weight over the balls of his feet. He may feel too close to the ball to start with, but the results of straighter shots should soon convince him that the medicine is working.

Tall golfers who tend to lift their spines as they swing have exactly the opposite symptoms. Possibly in an effort to stop feeling they are stretching out for the ball, they often set up bent too far forwards (with a spine angle of say 40 degrees). This is not like Matt's crouching stance, for he was well balanced. In this case, the golfer tends to have a narrow stance, his knees are not flexed enough and his weight is forward on his toes.

As a result, to keep balanced on the back swing, he jerks his spine, which leads to his slice. Once again, he has to treat his posture. He needs to stand more upright with a slightly wider stance and well flexed knees. At first, he may tend to top the ball, but after a while his timing will improve and his slice should fade away.

Physique, your physique, can also be a cause of your slice. It's not just a question of being short or tall, where the problem is really bad posture, it's whether you are slightly built or have a much fuller figure. Both can be contributory factors, but neither need lead to a permanent affliction.

The slightly built golfer who does not have much strength in hands or wrists is often a *weak swinger*. He (or she, as many senior ladies come in this category) tends to stand upright and swing upright too, to ease the physical pressure on stomach and hands. As a result he doesn't coil in the backswing and comes down on a steep out to in path, while his weak hand action ensures a short, high slice.

Such a swinger has to develop a more rotary swing and if he cannot physically swish through the ball any quicker, he must try at least to square the clubhead at impact. One treatment is to ensure that he plays with lightweight clubs and sets up less upright (like the shorter player) with less flex in the knees and the weight further forward. After takeaway, he must make an effort to cock the wrists fully before swinging the arms down on the inside.

A slight change of grip could also help to speed up hand action. This is the medicine prescribed for Brian, the slightest, senior member of our fourball. While not swinging too upright (because he strives for a draw for distance and so sets up closed and swings back quite flat) he has a weak hand action which sends the ball off right of target, to curve further right. Brian (and many others) should realise that it would be far better for them to adopt a strong grip. Many top women pros use a three knuckle grip very effectively, as they know they lack sheer strength. As weak swingers also tend to grab the club too tightly to raise it, which locks the wrists, Brian should also ease up on his grip pressure, especially with his right hand.

The bulky golfer equally has got a problem when it comes to coiling properly on the backswing. If you are a heavyweight with a large chest and waist and muscular arms, you could well belong to the last (but not least) category of slicer: the *shoulder shover*. If you are such a swinger, it's simply because you're not too supple and you find it hard to turn your shoulders sufficiently. As a result, you swing back very flat (the most common fault among the heavies) from an open stance (which you probably adopted to see where you are trying to hit the ball). Now because your arms finished the backswing moving

**TOO STEEP AN ARC FOR A WEAK SWINGER.**

around rather than up, they recoil into the downswing moving out and you shove with your shoulders to get some power into the shot. So you tend to hit it short, left to right, pulling your short irons and occasionally shanking one.

But don't despair. Some sterling heavyweights (Billy Caspar and Craig Stadler to name a formidable duo) have amply demonstrated that extra poundage does not restrict good golf. First, you will have to guard against setting up open: particularly with your build, it restricts the backswing, so set up slightly closed. Then you must bend over more from the hips, taking care not to have too much weight forward on your toes. This will promote a fuller wind up (standing closed) and a more upright swing (bending forward) as your shoulders will tilt more on the backswing.

You need to swing back slowly. But how far back? The fact is that your natural instincts will tell you how far to go. Some people will always have too long a swing, some people will always struggle to get to the horizontal. There is nothing wrong with a three-quarter backswing, which could suit many golfers who only play on weekends. You could combine it with a stronger grip, swing your arms down fast, aim for a high finish . . . and you could soon be hitting a long, controlled draw.

As you are easing your affliction (hopefully taking your medicine out on the practice ground) you will, as a confirmed golfer, still want to play. When you tee up though, do remember that curing a deep rooted affliction takes time. So use your head and give yourself a chance with the long shots. Tee your ball up high on the right of the tee and aim towards the left side of the fairway. Then at least you should be in play if the odd shot curls right. If others curve in the opposite direction, as they very well could, it will make a change searching for them in the left light rough.

## Hook as You Stand

These teeing up tactics won't do at all however for the hookers of the world. This minority group suffers in many ways from a more pernicious affliction, as the ball that swings hard left is generally hit a lot harder and runs even deeper into trouble. Hookers also don't fall into such interesting categories as slicers, as there are basically only three reasons why they hook – and one can lead to the others. But first of all let's dispose of one misconception: anyone who hits the ball left of target, for it to spin further left, is not a hooker. He is a puller, with a slicer's out to in swing, who has simply closed the club face through the ball. The true hook stems from a closed club face it's true, but the swing path is from in to out, or in to along the target line.

Unlike the slicer, the hooker has no problems in swinging his arms down fast. Quite the reverse. His grip however can cause the problem. If your shots start out straight before hooking, especially if they fly low (so low, you tend to leave your driver in the bag) then you almost certainly have the wrong grip for your swing. It could be too strong, which you can easily check by swinging back to the shaft parallel position. Even if the club is aligned along the target line and its toe points up, if the back of your left hand, or the palm of your right, faces the sky, you're too strong.

You may also be gripping too lightly with your right hand. Now while a weak left wrist through impact can let the strong right hand roll over it, closing the club face, an overtight left hand grip can slow the butt of the club in the hitting area. A light right hand grip in combination (which makes the right wrist more flexible and active) can whip the club face closed, so you hook. Getting the grip pressure all right isn't easy. You can check its neutrality, but if you still suffer, try holding the club a little more in the palms of your hands. Thicker than standard grips could help you to do this.

The fact remains that it is easier to use clubs with loft; the easiest of all are the five, six and seven irons. Why? Because they're short in shaft and have plenty of loft. A driver, a one and two iron are the most difficult because they're the longest in shaft and with the least amount of loft. So it's very important to think and use the clubs at your disposal. Remember Bobby Locke, one of the greatest pound for pound players ever, drove with a club with a fair amount of loft on it, almost a 2-wood. He had a number one head cover on it, but that was just to fool the opposition. Peter Thomson won certainly two or three of his Open championships using a 3-wood off the tee. Why? Because the seaside links courses, the championship courses, were hard, fast, bouncy, runny and the drive was only a positional shot setting up the next stroke to the green. He knew he had to be on the fairway from the tee otherwise he was a 'dead duck', so he settled on a slightly shorter distance from the tee although the hardness of the ground and the run of the ball took him well above the average length a professional drives and he was one of the world's great players.

So many handicap players persist with a driver when they should think twice. They read articles extolling the virtues of certain clubs and having spent a lot of money buying one they are loathe not to use it. In fact they would do far better to use a club with loft because the great thing is to get the ball on the fairway then you can start to play golf. Driving has to be closely behind putting as the most important element in the game; or so we believe.

With cause and effect at work, many hookers like Doug in our fourball are just not prepared to change anything. Doug, who has a *very* strong grip, has tried different holds in the past but couldn't stick with any of them because it felt too uncomfortable. As a result, he (like others) aims right of target instinctively to stop the ball going left. This closed stance sets the ball too far back in the stance, which makes him swing too far inside and too flat. If the club face is square to the target, his long shots will fly right to left, while his medium irons are usually pushed straight out right. He is quite philosophical about it all, but his game could improve a great deal with just a little common sense.

Doug has to set up square, with the ball further forward in his stance. He can check his alignment and its results on the practice ground before his next round. If he's on his own, he could place a club parallel to the target line and stand with his toes almost touching it. This would help to alleviate his very inside backswing, but he really also has to weaken his grip a little to straighten things out.

The third cause of the dreaded hook, which often develops from a very inside backswing, is when the body gets in the way of the arms as they swing down. As the body does not clear (perhaps because it does not coil enough on the backswing) the arms are blocked and the wrists unhinge and rotate rapidly through impact, closing the club face.

This 'body in the way' condition can sometimes be caused deliberately by golfers who exaggerate the concept of hitting against a firm left side. It can also come from setting up closed, as the golfer feels he has already half completed his backswing and so does not fully turn his shoulders, which inhibits the turn of the left hip. More often though the position of the feet are the culprits.

If your left side feels over rigid through impact, check your feet. You could unwittingly have set up with a square left foot, while your right points well right, making your coil easier but building little torque. In addition, coming down, your left foot will stop your body clearing, stiffening the left side and blocking a free arm swing. Far better to point the left foot out a little down the fairway, clearing the way for a long, straight shot towards the flat.

# THE GAME PLAN

A great many golfers are captains of industry, senior executives or managers, at home in a business environment. They are used to setting a budget each year and creating a clear business plan. Each day they have to make tough decisions in the office, applying their expertise, creativity and common sense to tricky situations. Above all, at work, they try to avoid mistakes, for these can be very costly.

Yet these same people ignore all their background experience and ability in planning carefully and taking rational decisions the moment they step onto a golf course. They invariably over estimate their capabilities (getting into deep trouble when trying to avoid a hazard too far away for them to reach). Or they take risks (trying to pull off a once in a lifetime shot over a lake that even a Tour pro wouldn't take on). They never seem to have any plan of action (treating each hole as if they were seeing it for the first time, despite having played it on many occasions). They don't take external factors into account (ignoring weather conditions) and they usually don't choose the most sensible option (playing the percentage shot to the heart of the green, instead of over a bunker). Above all, they make mistakes, which are more to do with indecision than ability (changing a five iron for a six and coming up woefully short).

Why do they do it? Is it a subconscious reaction to the pressures of the daily grind? Does it make them feel good to be *irresponsible*? One thing is sure: if they managed their business the way most of them play golf, they wouldn't last long in any company.

On the other hand, if they played golf the way they practise in management (planning ahead, weighing the risks, thinking positively) then the average social golfer's handicap would be 10 instead of 18.

For golf is a game of *course management*. Once its basics are understood, 90 per cent of the game is all to do with judgement and attitude. The trouble is that the vast majority of golfers only think about improving the 10 per cent (driving, iron shots, chipping, bunker play and putting) and ignore everything else, which they often are better equipped to handle. For learning to improve your swing, or your putting, requires a lot of effort and practice – but all golfers can improve the management of their game.

In fact, scoring far better with what you've got only needs the application of intelligence and common sense. You can easily prove this if you payed to play a round on your home course with your local pro, asking him to advise you on every shot as for the right club, direction and the shot ahead – rather than technique. If then you can master the non-technical aspects of the game and improve your course management, as a high handicapper you could simply cut some 10 shots off your score every time you play.

# No More Guesswork

The first rule in course management is to know your capabilities, so you have to do an inventory of your assets. This means that you must *know* just how far you really hit each club, for without this you will never score consistently well. Now most golfers assume that they hit a 5-iron some 10 yards longer than they do a six, or a four 10 yards past a five, but this can be a fallacy, and much depends also on making a perfect strike each time. The only thing for it is to hit a series of balls with each club on the practice ground and be sure to note where each ball lands, because you must know how far you *carry* each shot.

You may be very surprised when you undertake this arduous, yet very rewarding, exercise. For even if conditions are good (dry, little wind, etc) as they should be, you will probably find you don't get the carry with each club that you thought you did (no wonder you buried the ball in so many bunkers in the past). On average, the club golfer will hit his driver at best some 230 yards, with a carry of about 180 yards on a dry, level field. He will hit his 3-wood some 200 yards, with a carry of 160, while his 5-wood (or 3-iron) will carry 160 yards, rolling a further 20 or so.

The other irons probably each hit some 10 yards less, with a decreasing amount of roll, 'around' the 5-iron, which should carry about 135 yards, rolling another 15. But pay special attention to the distance you really get with your 9-iron and pitching wedge. You won't hit the wedge *consistently* over 90 yards on target and you would be unlikely to strike your sand iron over 65 yards under good conditions. But you have to know your best distances (to make allowances in difficult situations) and once the guesswork has gone out of your game, just watch your scores come down as your confidence goes up.

You must though leave nothing to chance. You have to know all the relevant background details before you can create a business plan (size of market, types of consumers, distribution costs, etc). So you must equally *know* the details of the course you are going to play. You must know where the out-of-bounds are, the distances of bunkers from the tee or green, the local rules, the depths of the greens – everything relevant that might affect your play.

Tour pros (and/or their caddies) do this meticulously before every tournament, using measuring wheels or pacing out the distances on practice rounds. You don't have to go as far as that, but you really ought to have the vital background data of your own home course fully logged. It is not difficult to compile an easy to carry map of the course; you can note the key distances that most influence your shots as you play your next few rounds. And pay particular attention to the distances to hazards from the tee and the amount of room you have to work with around (and behind) each green. These are not often noted in the guides you can buy to popular courses, but the fact that these guides exist should also tell you something. They are not called 'strokesavers' for nothing.

Once armed with all this important background data, you are almost ready to plan to do business on the golf course. But before you start, there is a regular, routine preparation to attend to which will also boost your confidence that you've left nothing to chance. You must first check your equipment. Are your clubs clean, or are the grooves in the irons filled with caked mud and grass? It may make little difference to backspin, but psychologically you feel more of a golfer when you set a gleaming club face against a new ball. And how

CHART EVERY HOLE ON YOUR HOME COURSE.

about the grips: are they dry or tacky? A quick clean before you play will make each club feel in top condition – and you too.

Then there's your shoes. If they were soaked the last time, did you dry them out carefully (not on a radiator) and are any of the spikes missing or worn? Uncomfortable footwear can be very disrupting, so take a little care. The same applies to clothes. You must be sure your rig of the day will keep you comfortable. Temperatures can change a great deal, winds can blow up and rain can fall, both winter and summer, so you have to be prepared. No pro will set out on a tournament round without a spare sweater, an umbrella and a reliable set of waterproofs, as well as a hat of some kind. Nobody likes a wet head, or rain trickling down the neck.

All this preparation, which is little more than common sense, helps to reinforce a positive attitude, but a large majority of golfers scorn it. As a result, where they should be alert and focused on managing their game, they are often uncomfortable and unsure of what they are doing. So they only think about the 10 per cent of golf, the technical aspects of their swings, and multiply the mistakes, scoring heavily. Our fourball is no exception. Let's see how they tackled the short fifteenth.

This is a relatively innocuous par four, some 390 yards long, with a flat, wide fairway. A drainage ditch runs along in the right hand rough for part of the way and there is a dense copse of pine trees on the left, although both are well clear of the fairway. There is only one shallow fairway bunker a good 240 yards out from the tee on the left, while two greenside bunkers (left and right) guard the putting surface. Aside from a slope of thickish rough at the back of the green, that's all.

So how did our four cope? Were they fighting for birdies, while making sure of their pars? Well, Doug (with the honour) took his driver and smashed a horrendous hook deep into the copse, some 220 yards from the tee. His partner Bob, seeing the ball disappear and feeling he at least had to be long down the middle, sliced dreadfully over the rough into the drainage ditch. Matt and Brian, a little smugly, then played their drives down the fairway, 210 and 190 yards from the tee and safely on the right.

Doug found his ball among the trees, but tried to scoop it out through too narrow a gap, ricocheted off a branch and ended up in a worse place, with no backswing. He did manage though to poke his third shot out onto the very edge of the trees. Slightly blocked from the green, he then tried to hook his fourth onto the green, but aiming well right, the ball flew straight into the rough, pin high.

Bob hasn't seen any of this, being the other side of the fairway as well as being the shortest off the tee and so first to play. Pulling his ball out of the ditch and dropping it a couple of clublengths away though, he realises that he needs a peach of a shot to get to the green, some 210 yards away. So he strikes hard with his 3-wood and almost pulls it off. His ball ends in the right greenside bunker.

Brian, playing next, is very sensible. From the fairway, he plays his 3-wood and it is unfortunate that it just curls into the right rough some 30 yards from the green. Matt, however, feels he can easily reach as he has only 180 yards to go. So he pulls out his 3-iron, intending to hit it firmly. But he doesn't notice that his ball is sitting down a little on the fairway and so he only thins it about 100 yards. Fuming as he approaches it, he then isn't sure which club to take for the remaining 80 yards (is it 80? Or more like 90?). He picks his pitching wedge, hesitates, then 'to be sure' settles for his 9-iron. His ball, well struck, pitches past the pin and bounds off the green into the thick rough behind.

As they approach the flag, Brian is faced with a tricky shot as the hole lies over the right hand bunker. He could reach the putting surface on the left without too much difficulty, but it would be a long way from the hole and he hasn't been putting all that well (having told himself on the second that it was going to be 'one of those days' on the greens). So he tries to play a high, soft pitch just over the bunker from the rough – and ends up in the sand near Bob's ball.

Doug next pitches out of the rough, his fifth shot running well past the hole, and two putts for a most inglorious seven. He is joined shortly by Matt, whose pitch from the thick rough at the back just reaches the edge of it. His chip also runs past and his first putt rims the hole, but stays out giving him another triple-bogey. Bob, determined to do better, takes far too much sand with his fourth shot, barely moving the ball forwards. But he manages to splash his fifth some ten feet from the hole and, inspired putter that he is, sinks the next for a six. Brian, white knuckled, follows him out of the bunker in one, but then two putts, halving the hole. But the final score of two sevens and two sixes really is a little appalling, and if the four of them had each used a little thought, they could have shaved many shots off the total.

For example, when Doug stood on the tee he was very aware of the left hand fairway bunker, which would trap his ball if he hit his best, long draw. So he aimed well right and hooked. If he had taken his 3-wood and swung smoothly, there was no chance he would have found the sand. Also, when he was deep in the woods, he should have picked the widest gap (even if it meant hitting backwards) just to get out onto the fairway.

Matt made his errors playing off the fairway. He did not check the lie of his ball and tried to force a 3-iron when a 5-wood would have been the better club. He also did not know his distance to the flag and that made him indecisive, which is invariably bad.

Bob equally should have thought about the fairway bunker – and he should have known that even his best drive would never have reached it. So he should have aimed directly at it: with his natural slice, he would probably have ended up in the middle of the fairway. In the right rough though, with 210 yards to go, he should not have played a career best shot. He should have thought about laying up. An 8-iron from the rough would have left him with an easy pitching wedge to the green and he might have put it close enough to make a decent bogey.

Of all of them, Brian played the hole the most sensibly – and could/should have won it instead of halving. He only made one mistake: he did not play the percentage shot to the green when short of it in the rough. He should have looked closely at the area he had to land the ball in between bunker and flag. The green is long, but not too wide and if Brian had been honest he would have given himself a 30 per cent chance of making the shot. That is to say that with the amount of difficulty in hitting the ball softly from the rough and stopping it near the hole, he would have dumped it in the bunker three times out of ten, fluffed it just out of the rough twice, gone too far over the green twice out of ten as well – and only made the shot, at best, three times. On the other hand, if he had aimed well clear of the bunker for the fat of the green, he would have been on the putting surface about eight times out of ten, an 80 per cent chance. Had he then two putted, he would have made bogey, which would have won the hole.

That is not to say that Brian should *always* take a cautious approach and play the best percentage shot all the time. Had the match been all square at the eighteenth, for example, he most certainly should have had a go. But generally all club golfers would score a lot better if they weighed the options before attempting anything. This was not a very difficult par four. There are many others that are much more challenging and yet they can be parred, or birdied, by a golfer who does not have exceptional length or accuracy, but who does have a clear game plan before

**ALWAYS PLAY THE PERCENTAGES.**

he tees off and applies sensible tactics should he find himself in a little difficulty.

## Tactics from Green to Tee

So how do you devise a game plan for any hole, rather than simply surveying it from the tee and deciding to hit it right, or left, to avoid a hazard? Well, you could do worse than to take a leaf out of the book of Peter Thomson, the cheerful, confident Australian, who won five British Opens between 1954 and 1965.

At his peak, Thomson had a simple, compact swing and always played well within himself. He was usually outdriven by most of his peers, yet this never bothered him unduly. He has said: "The most important facets of golf are careful planning, calm and clear thinking and the ordinary logic of common sense. Golf calls for logical observation. Beyond that the big thing is not power, but judgement."

He always had a game plan for the day and he always stuck to it unless he saw a rare opportunity to make a telling shot, which helped him to win many a tournament. He analysed every hole carefully, charting the hazards, working out angles and distances, allowing for different wind and weather conditions. He also planned how he would play each hole *backwards*, that is to say he decided where he would like to end up on the green, and then chose the best angle and distance off to achieve it, which depended on his own ability, with a certain margin of error. This pinpointed the area where he should hit his drive, rather than him making that decision when standing on the tee.

If you, as a club golfer, don't want to think backwards like Thomson, you still need to have a clear plan in mind as to how you will tackle any hole before you start your pre-shot routine on the tee. From the tee, you must consider three things: the club you need (for the distance you must carry the ball and where it will roll to), the weather conditions (especially the wind) and where the worst trouble lies. All three, in many cases, are interdependent.

Knowing how far you hit each club and whether you normally fade (or slice) it takes care of a part of the equation. But the wind conditions, which vary constantly, do need careful thought. If you

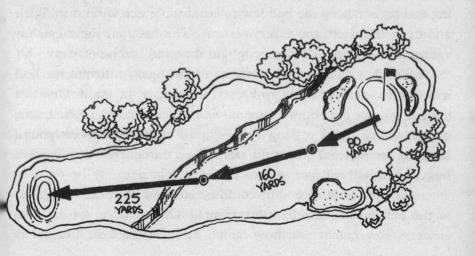

PLANNING BACKWARDS CAN CUT SHOTS.

have to play into a headwind, try and keep the ball low (as if it balloons up it will slice or hook more severely) and expect very little roll. So take a stronger club than you normally would, grip a little down it, set the hands forward of the clubhead and hit the ball with a three-quarter punch.

Downwind, you must not try and slam the ball extra hard. You should tee it well up and make a full, smooth swing, letting the wind do the work. But you will gain extra distance (so really look hard at the hazards) plus accuracy, as the wind tends to straighten out slice or hook.

Crosswinds can be very contrary. A left to righter is not too bad for the hook: you can aim straight where you want to end up and let the wind straighten it out. But if you slice, you have to aim off well left and try and keep the ball low to avoid too much wind drift. With a right to left wind, the reverse is true. The habitual slicer can for once aim straight, as his slice will fight the wind and he may even hit the ball further. The hooker should aim right, again punching the ball with a three-quarter swing to keep it low under the wind. One last thing: if you are not entirely sure of wind effect, strength or direction, it's not much good tossing bits of grass in the air when you're standing on the tee. Look at the trees down the course instead: don't forget, your ball will rise at least to tree-top height.

Gauging how your shot could be affected by conditions leads to the next main consideration: trouble. On each tee you have to estimate how potent and how far off each hazard lies. An out-of-bounds, a two shot hazard (stroke and distance) must be avoided at all cost, as should a thick copse of trees, which could involve you not just in a lost ball, but with much scuffling among the roots. Lakes, streams, ditches and fairway bunkers, all one shot hazards, must also be avoided. But you must *know* just how far they lie off the tee. If you can't reach them with your Sunday best shot, it could make sense to play towards them and so avoid other less obvious trouble.

But don't dwell on any hazards: the more you think about them, the more likely you are to end up in them. So remember to hit away from trouble at all times.

Finally, on the tee, when you've made up your mind how the wind will affect your shot, where you will aim for to avoid the worst trouble and hence which club you'll hit to get the right carry and roll, don't change it. You must concentrate on the shot: go into your pre-shot routine focused on striking the ball well – and never try too hard to force or press.

If, despite careful planning and execution, you miss the fairway and find your ball in the deep rough you will only have one option.

You have to get out of it and onto the fairway by the safest possible route. You must not be greedy; just take your wedge and pitch out. And if you're in the light stuff and a long from the green, don't be greedy either. More shots are thrown away like that as you tend to swing extra hard to get the distance and fail to hit the ball squarely, crisp and clean.

In the woods you have to keep very calm. Do not try to smash the ball out, thinking you can bend branches (it's amazing how a pencil thin twig can deflect a ball backwards). Equally don't try to gain a lot of distance to (or even hit) the green if you have to thread the ball through several tree trunks. You may have read some pros advice to aim at the edge of the nearest tree, but ignore that. Just aim for the most appropriate gap and play firmly towards (and hopefully through) it.

What makes an appropriate gap? Well, it should be at least three feet wide if your ball is lying six feet away. At ten feet, it must be some six feet wide, and twenty feet into the woods needs at least a ten foot gap to be sure of getting out. Never forget, you are not Seve Ballesteros – although, like Seve, *around* the fairway, you have to be very aware of the rules of the game, which can bring relief from trouble. Remember that the 'embedded ball' rule works 'through the green', which means in the rough. Remember also the relief you get from the scrapings of 'burrowing animals' (although Seve failed to prove this case in the 1994 Volvo Masters on the critical last hole).

On the fairway, all the factors you take into account on the tee also apply, plus a few others. Supposing you've followed your game plan and hit a good drive onto the fairway, which gives you a good angle into the green. You've managed to cope with the wind and you know how far it is to the flag and the carry over any water or bunkers. But is the green holding, or are its approaches hard and dry? And is the fairway itself soft from too much rain?

GO FOR A GOOD GAP IN THE WOODS.

Water and mud can make a clean strike difficult and you may have to take a more lofted club, sacrificing distance, to make sure of catching the ball squarely. In really wintry conditions the ball doesn't travel as far through the heavier air, so you need to take a stronger club than you normally would. The green though would be holding well, unless it was frosty, so you must consider that too.

You also must think sometimes about laying up, something club golfers rarely do. With tough par four holes, the additional pressure of trying to aim for the green can lead to a lot of trouble: far better to be placed a full sand iron distance from the flag. You should also be prepared to lay up in front of water, as many top pros (and winners) do in the Augusta Masters. This is where your judgement of the best percentage shot comes into play – and, in the worst conditions, the safest shot is always the best one to play.

The lie of your ball on the fairway is also very important, as it can really influence direction – something which many club golfers, despite having played for years, fail to appreciate. If you are standing with your right foot above your left on a downhill lie, you need to select a more lofted club as a 6-iron will play more like a five, the slope cancelling out some of the loft. You then need to keep your weight on your left side, play the ball more off your right foot and aim left of the target. On an uphill lie, you have the reverse situation. You must take a less lofted club, lean a little into the slope and play the ball nearer your left foot so that the club strikes it at the bottom of the arc.

On a sidehill lie, when the ball is below your feet, it will tend to slice. So you must set up aiming left, standing close with a full length grip and your weight slightly back on your heels. If the ball is above your feet it will tend to hook. So stand a little further from the ball, grip down the shaft, weight on the balls of your feet and aim right of target. With all these shots though don't be too ambitious with length. You must avoid lunging at the ball at all costs and losing your balance. You should also take a few practice swings *in situ*, just to get the feel of how you should balance and swing.

But all this comes under the 'planning for emergencies' side of course management. Far better if you can avoid woods, water, and sand altogether and plan to hit your fairway shots from level lies. Tackling the par threes, fours and fives with this in mind from the start is the way to really cut shots off your score, rather than scrambling your way around.

## Score on the Odd Pars

A good par three hole should always pose a challenge to the golfer, but it should also offer every golfer a chance to score at worst a par. It is very important to get your pars here and on the par fives. With four threes and four fives marked on your card, the par fours will do you less damage. On the tee, you have everything going for you. You are playing with the ball teed up, hitting a precisely known distance and you can usually see all the hazards clearly.

In most cases, your teeing tactics are important. Always use a tee peg as you want to be certain of hitting the ball before the ground and if the flag is on the left side of the green hit from the right side of the teeing area, as that gives you the best line in to it. The reverse is true if the flag's on the right – but often you should consider playing to the heart of the green if the pin is tucked away behind a nasty bunker.

If one of the par threes has an elevated green, plan to take a stronger club than you would normally use for that distance. The ball will not travel so far because the elevated green reduces the parabola of the shot. It's exactly the opposite when you're playing from an elevated tee to a green far below. In this case, use one club less because the extra drop extends the parabola.

Should you ever think of laying up on a par three? It might make sense if there is a large pond lurking in front of the flag and the carry is more than 150 yards. In this case, the social golfer has a better option of making par if he aims left or right of the water, giving himself a good chance of pitching close. And don't be influenced by the scornful attitude of your opponents: they could soon change it if they drive too far over the green or splash into the pond.

With the par fours, long or short, your first priority is to hit the fairway. Remember that if a stream or a cluster of fairway bunkers lie 240 yards off the tee and your best drive is only 230 yards, it is usually the best tactics to aim at them. When you're safely on the fairway though, the long holes (from 430–470 yards) are often beyond the range of most club golfers in two shots. So you must plan beforehand to lay up: to leave the ball on a level lie in a position where you can make a pitch that will leave you the simplest putt for par. *Don't* just take a 3-wood and slam away: you will almost certainly find yourself struggling to make bogey.

You can however consider the par fives as holes that give you one extra chance to recover – and still make par, if not a birdie.

On the tee, with a dog-leg hole as many are, the golfer is often tempted to go for the big, high shot over the trees, cutting off yards from the dog-leg and . . . *don't*. All par fives can be played sensibly, laying up for the third shot, which gives you a chance for a pitch and one putt. So plan a safe area in which to land your drive, resist the temptation of threading a long, long shot around overhanging trees to carry deep greenside bunkers, and instead pick out a level area from which you can pitch close to the flag. Remember that most par fives are designed with fewer hazards than par fours (their length providing the great difficulty for most golfers) and that the closer your ball comes to rest by that hazard, the easier your next shot will be. That's what your game plan for the course should highlight: it must put you in a position to play the easiest next shot, always.

## Never Give Up

From the start you must plan the way you approach the game you are about to play. Unfortunately many people don't: typically, they rush up to the club in a hurry without any time to do more than take a few practice swings, let alone spend ten minutes hitting half-a-dozen balls to break down the adhesions.

One of the curses of golf is that it does take a long time. Squash and tennis are quickfire games and you can get a lot of exercise from them in thirty minutes or so. But not with golf. It's a slow, pedestrian affair and you must approach it sensibly. Before you play again, you must be sure your clubs are right and

PLAYING A RIGHT DOG-LEG, AIM LEFT.

that your swing is reasonably consistent. If you feel you need a lesson or two from your local pro, have half-a-dozen and 'pack them in' as quickly as you can to retain and build on your coach's wise words. Give yourself time to warm up before you play. Get as many things right as you can *before* you start – and this includes deciding on a clear game plan, which you must try and stick to with the best of your ability.

But the best laid plans can go very wrong if you have the wrong attitude to the glorious game. The trouble is that when a golfer hits a few good shots in a row, his confidence rises, he starts to hum cheerfully and he relaxes and swings well.

All it takes though is a couple of bad shots consecutively and the skies darken. His confidence level drops like a stone, he tenses up and starts hacking from trouble to even deeper trouble. What is worse, is that his negative attitude lasts much longer than his positive one – unless he guards against it and tries to be positive (and cheerful) no matter what.

If you hit a bad patch, hitting behind the ball and half topping it a hundred yards, then seeing your ball bounce sideways into a bunker on your next one, *stop* and think clearly. You should not let your confidence wither away. Both shots were within half an inch of being good ones – and your next shot could well be excellent.

Those of you who also tend to give up if you start the round badly, as so many do, there is at least one splendid example to help you view the remainder of your round positively. It was, in addition, set by a golfer in the Captain's Day Competition on his home course. Alan Telford, a ten handicapper, started *very* badly. He took a 7 on the first, which was a par three. Just think: four of his allotted shots had gone in the first five minutes. Yet Telford had the ability to look on each shot and each hole as a separate issue.

Quietly determined, he put the disaster on the first out of his mind. He then birdied the second and made very few mistakes in the rest of his round, finishing with a net 67, which was good enough to win the competition.

That is the example to keep in mind if your game plan goes awry, but you must make a clear game plan as soon as possible. It will help you to shave many shots off your score.

# MATCHPLAY: THE LAZY GOLFER'S GAME

I t is extraordinary that the most popular form of golf, played by millions of golfers worldwide, matchplay, is only seen in a few professional tournaments, and that not every year. The World Matchplay (whatever its sponsor), the Walker and Ryder Cups (and the Curtis and Solheim Cups for women) provide rare opportunities for a golfer to view the game that matters most to him, or her.

The problem is that although matchplay is the finest form of the game, many pros dislike it. They hate being beaten in the first round, while in a stroke play event they could always finish strongly, with a rush of birdies, to end up high on the list. In stroke play, finishing second counts (a lot, with current prize money) but in matchplay, finishing second counts for nothing.

It is true that in some major stroke play tournaments there have been absorbing 'head to head' duels over the last nine holes. The British Open has produced some memorable encounters, like Jacklin v Trevino in 1972, and Nicklaus v Watson five years later.

Yet in these cases, as in many of the notable play-offs for other majors, like the US Opens, the protagonists were playing the course and not each other. So it is hard for the viewing golfer to appreciate any matchplay tactics employed, to learn from them the cut and thrust of play that lies at the heart of his weekly game.

But tactics there are, as there are (and always have been) some golfers who have shone at matchplay. Walter Hagan, Gary Player and Seve Ballesteros have blazed down the years to the 1990s. Hagan won five US PGAs in the 1920s (then head to head 36 hole matches) and beat the best of the world, including Bobby Jones, in other matchplay events. Player has to-date won the World Matchplay Championship more often than anyone else, and has some of the most memorable 'come backs' to his credit. Ballesteros has won almost as many Matchplays as Player, and has been the inspiration of European Ryder Cup victories. Each has embodied what it takes to be a champion at this form of golf: sheer determination, the ability to recover from difficult situations, to play a telling shot at the key phase of a match, to come from behind, and above all the absolute will to win.

## Win Slowly

There are many lessons the club golfer can learn from these (and other) matchplay experts, which will improve their regular weekly game. They are all about strategy and tactics, which have the same basic approach whether playing singles (or a three ball) or when playing with a partner in a fourball, foursome or greensome.

In a matchplay singles, the first thing the social golfer must appreciate is that he is in for a *mental* battle. Never mind if he is playing a friendly game for a couple of balls or the drinks, nobody likes to lose. The objective is to win, fair and square, hopefully enjoying the play. If it is a friendly, the 'rules of engagement' should be amiable (no long debates on whether it is, or isn't, casual water etc) but you are trying to *win* the match. So the more prepared you are for it, the better.

This means that you arrive at the first tee well equipped, nicely warmed up and with a clear plan of the distances and hazards of each hole at your command. But you must not start by attacking course and man furiously in an immediate effort to get one up. Just get your drive in play. Don't hammer your approach at the flag, try and get it somewhere on the green – and be content to get down in two putts. You have to pace your effort through the match and the time to attack may come later. The worst thing is to take a bogey or double bogey at the start by trying too hard, find yourself one down and in trying to pull back struggle into further trouble.

Whatever some pundits might say though, you have to play the *man* and not just the course. But playing him by playing your own game, is not the same as trying to outplay him. Peter Thomson learned this lesson (and a great deal about matchplay) when he played Bobby Locke in a series of 47 matches in South Africa in 1956. Locke won 11 out of the first 14 matches before Thomson realised what was happening. "I was trying to beat him and he just sat back and let me beat myself" he said. "I was trying to out-drive him, out-approach him and out-putt him. It was all too much of a strain and I succeeded in nothing."

So Thomson decided to change his strategy. Instead of forcing, struggling to come from behind, he relaxed and simply tried to play safely. He gave away no holes impetuously, but made Locke earn every one . . . and suddenly he started to win. In fact, he won or tied the next matches until they were level, although Locke managed to get ahead 22 to 21 at the end.

The lesson for the club golfer is clear, particularly when it comes to trying to out-drive an opponent. If you find yourself up against a player who hits the ball a lot further than you do, don't try to out-muscle him, or even keep up with him. It puts too much pressure on you. In fact, the pressure could well be on him. As the longer hitter, he is supposed to out-distance you by far from off the tee, which should give him an edge, but to achieve this on every hole can lead to mistakes. You will also be hitting your approach shots first and if you can put these on the green, never mind near the flag, the pressure builds on him to get inside you.

You can however throw it all away and put an insidious pressure on yourself if you lose a hole to par, especially when your opponent is in trouble off the tee. This can stop any fight back you may be making dead in its tracks and often lose you the match there and then. It was the crucial point in the 1994 Toyota World Matchplay Championship final at Wentworth between Colin Montgomerie,

**DON'T LET A LONG HITTER WORRY YOU.**

Europe's leading money winner for the season, and Ernie Els of South Africa, who was the '94 US Open champion.

They ended the morning round all square and in the afternoon Els was two up when they came to the par four fifteenth, although Montgomerie was hanging on well and there was everything to play for. Then Els pulled his drive, ending up in a fairway bunker. He was in double trouble: he was well up the face of the bunker and when he got out should have been left with a long third shot to the green. Montgomerie just had to find the fairway, aiming then to play safely to the green for a par and a win. One down and three to play is not too bad in the cauldron of Wentworth and many matches have been won there from worse positions.

At this key moment though, Montgomerie, almost unbelievably, followed Els into the same fairway bunker, his ball ending even further up the face. He lost the hole in the end to a par – and the match was all over at the next hole. A amateur in that situation should have made *sure* of getting on the fairway, even if it meant taking a three or four iron off the tee. You must never lose an easy hole to par and, above all, throw away a hole your opponent is handing you on a plate. Elementary mistakes are often the most costly: they make all the difference between winning and losing.

You can also throw it all away if you take an unnecessary chance on a shot when you're ahead in a match. When you're up, going for the spectacular shot, the extra-long carry over a bunker near the flag, just is not on. Bobby Jones learned this lesson when

**DON'T GO FOR THE SPECTACULAR SHOT.**

playing for the US Amateur Championship in 1921. Two up on the eighth in his match against the British champion of the day, Willie Hunter, he tried to cut a dog-leg by carrying his drive over some trees. It was a shot he had played before with success, but this time his ball caught a top branch and fell into a ditch full of stones and weeds, from which he failed to extract it first time. He lost the hole to a par, the match on the seventeenth and knew ruefully that the eighth was the turning point. He had taken the chance, instead of making his opponent take it.

For indeed the one time you should take a chance, go for a spectacular recovery shot or flirt with water or sand, is when you are behind. When it is the last resort, when holes are running out, then you should try. But be aware, these shots rarely succeed.

## Seven Mistakes a Round

Another powerful weapon in the armoury of a good matchplay golfer is a calm, unruffled temperament. He never lets himself get upset by his opponent, the rubs of the green, or his own bad shots. The classic exponent of this precept was Walter Hagan, who won 11 majors in his time. With it, he beat Bobby Jones on the only occasion they played head to head, over 72 holes in 1926, by 11 and 10.

Hagan played some terrible shots by all accounts, but followed them up with brilliant escapes and with a red hot putter (sinking 'one of them') broke his opponent's morale.

Hagan blithely accepted that when he started a match he only had his game of that day, not the one of the week before, nor the one he might have the following month. So he had to make the best of what he had, which is why he avoided paralysis by any attempt at analysis. He also said he *expected* to make at least seven mistakes every round and so if he hit a bad shot he never worried about it, as it was just one of the seven.

He was also totally unconcerned about missing even short putts, feeling that it was impossible to roll the ball over uncertain ground with any regularity. So he just concentrated on making the next one, without thinking that perhaps his putting stroke might be wrong. Above all, he accepted good and bad luck as an integral part of the game, which is a great maxim for the lazy golfer.

It helps, to diminish mental tension, which can grab and demolish any golfer. Faced with an intimidating carry over water say, even if your opponent has landed in trouble, most of us feel tense and anxious. The club is gripped too tightly, the swing shortens and speeds up and a bad shot is often guaranteed. In this case, you should take the longest club necessary to get well over the hazard, concentrating only on where you would land the ball on the far side.

Were you to be in a similar position as Colin Montgomerie however, with your opponent in a fairway bunker a long way off the tee, then you should take a club which would never reach it under any circumstances and play the shot in a calm frame of mind. Facing the need to 'just get a par', you must play the safest shot you can and be prepared to take the 'rub of the green'. But it is very difficult at matchplay not to be jolted by a possibly lucky shot from your opponent, particularly if it comes at an important psychological moment in the match. This happened to Jack Nicklaus in his famous last round duel with Tom Watson in the 1977 British Open. All right, it wasn't matchplay, but it was the most magical head to head encounter in every sense of the word.

They were both level after three rounds (having each scored 65s in the third) and came to the fifteenth green on the last day in scenes of tremendous crowd excitement. Nicklaus was some fourteen feet from the hole, while Watson was off the green some seven or eight feet. But Watson holed out. It was a body blow for Nicklaus; a wicked punch coming at a key moment and probably it was then Nicklaus knew this was not going to be his Open, although he never gave up trying. And who will ever forget the sensational last hole, the 72nd, which was halved in three?

## Nerves and Jitters

If you are not super-human, then you are bound to be affected by a 'lucky' shot by your opponent – but you should try very hard not to be unduly influenced by his behaviour otherwise. There is quite a lot of bluff around in matchplay and many players, amateurs as well as pros, are very adept at psyching out their opposition.

Walter Hagan, needless to say, enjoyed a good bluff. In the 1927 US PGA, playing Joe Turnesa, he came to the last hole all square. There, with Turnesa in good position in the middle of the fairway, Hagan pushed his approach shot into some tall grass, partially screened from the green by trees. Hagan then started to 'bluff'. The gap through the trees was quite wide, but Turnesa didn't know that. Hagan walked up and down several times studying his line to the green, selected and rejected different clubs, and finally waved his opponent back, saying he might have to play it safe. Then he hit his shot to within twelve feet of the flag. Turnesa, who had been kept waiting for quite a time watching the 'performance', must have been affected by such a 'miracle' shot, for he hit his easy one into a greenside bunker – and Hagan won his fifth PGA.

Now while such a performance is over the top and never really seen today, some golfers occasionally stoop to bluff, like hitting an easy 7-iron, and letting their opponent see the club, when an 8- would be the right one. Others go further into unacceptable gamesmanship.

Not any members of our fourball, of course. Being good friends they would never dream of adopting such tactics. Occasionally, it's true, Doug has been annoyed at Matt for 'shuffling about' on the tee when he (Doug) was about to drive. On other occasions Brian has suspected Bob of replacing his ball on the green nearer the hole than his marker indicated, while they all sometimes thought Brian had failed to count an extra bunker shot or two. But these are more

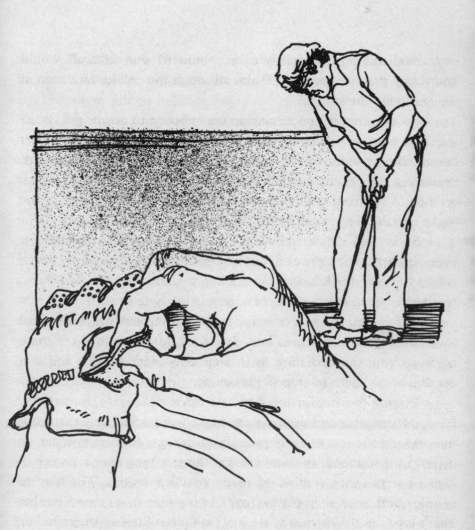

DON'T GET DISTRACTED BY 'GAMESMANSHIP'.

*suspicions*, unintended annoyances. None of our fourball would knowingly practice gamesmanship, although they all know a man at the club who does.

So just what is gamesmanship (as opposed to downright cheating) and how do you counter the main ploys? Well, Stephen Potter has amusingly outlined a few in 'Golfmanship' (invoking sympathy, proffering advice, and wearing the absolutely correct clothes) which are not so far from reality. But they are nowhere near some of the tricks certain players (including Tour pros) practice.

Some will deliberately make a distracting noise (clanking a club, ripping open a glove) to put an opponent off as he putts, which comes too near the knuckle. Others might stand near the right hand tee marker when their opponent is getting ready to drive, making him wonder if his grip, stance, or swing is being analysed, which can lead to unsettling self-awareness and doubt. Should someone try these ploys on you, the best thing is to step away with a smile and if it continues ask them to stop it, pleasantly.

Playing too fast, or too slow, are other deliberate distractions. An opponent who hurries along can make you instinctively rush your own judgement and shots, to your disadvantage. Equally, you can be driven to distraction by someone who lingers long over a choice of club or a pre-shot routine of many practice swings. The way to counter both is to keep playing your own game at your own tempo. Don't try to out-slow your adversary (as Curtis Strange suggested he would do when he thought he and Tom Kite would be drawn against

Bernhard Langer and Ken Brown in the 1987 Ryder Cup) and don't try to play faster than him either.

Sometimes though an opponent, wrapped up in a cocoon of concentration, will start to walk off the tee almost before you've completed your drive. Or else he will walk well ahead of you in the rough when you still have to play your approach to the green. Are these ploys? They can distract, if you let them, but you should try not to hit him with your second shot.

Above all, you should never be afraid to ask him nicely to stop doing whatever he's doing that distracts you. This is also the only response to one very popular ploy, where an opponent is always getting in your peripheral vision, taking a practice shot or three, as you are preparing to putt. Have none of that. Step away, ask him to move well clear and start all over again. Whatever you do never play a gamesman at his own game, play him at yours.

## Playing as a Team

Sound matchplay tactics are equally important when you play in a fourball or foursomes game. You have to know your partner's strengths and play to them (as he does to yours) and planning a game strategy before you start certainly helps. For example, the steadier, if shorter, driver should plan to play first at the more difficult holes, which gives his partner more freedom and less tension to swing when it's his turn. When club golfers play however, they rarely think of the holes ahead.

One of the team will take the honour because he feels it's 'his turn'. If it's Bob, say, and he lands in deep trouble, the pressure on his partner Doug is upped unnecessarily and he is more likely to make a bad tee shot.

Much the same applies on the fairway. The golfer who has to play first should concentrate on hitting his ball as safely as he can into a good position as near to the green as possible. This gives his partner the opportunity to attack the flag – and on most holes at least one member of a team should be able to play aggressively. Far too often though, at a club level, both members of a team play as if they were individuals, each one seemingly trying to make a birdie on every hole and ending up with both scoring bogey or double bogey.

A two-ball foursome is a great winter game. Played by relatively good players it's possible to finish 36 holes in a day. It is also a great test of character although it is not so popular with the club golfer. It is the fastest way to play golf, can be great fun and makes you very aware that you are only one member of a team. For its one essential is to hit your shot into a position which makes the next one easy for your partner. But it is also very important that you are both in agreement as to how you play any hole, when to take a chance, when to lay up. This should be done before you tee off, as long debates on the course must be avoided at all cost.

With both of a team's balls on the green (in a fourball) the player furthest from the hole must get his within tap-in range, if he can. His partner can then 'go for it' with confidence. Sometimes however it might be more tactical to reverse the order. If the player who is sinking everything that day is lying furthest from the hole, he might ask his partner to putt first to see how the ball rolls and to give himself a chance of getting down in one. But both should be aware of how their opponents lie. As with singles, you must try never to throw an easy hole away, never to lose one to a par – and you must be aware of the state of the match at all times.

Playing as part of a team means that you have to be aware of how your team is doing overall, because in matchplay it can sometimes help you to win. Bernhard Langer, a relentless matchplayer, has always been very alert to the main chance for his team. He showed this ability to the best in the 1987 Ryder Cup, which was played at Muirfield Village.

Coming to the eighteenth, playing Larry Nelson, the match was all square and both of them were lying some three feet from the hole, having putted up. Langer then looked at the scoreboard and saw that the overall match score was Europe 13 – US 12 and he knew that to retain the Cup, Europe only needed another point. He also saw that in the last match out on the course, the one behind them, Seve Ballesteros, was dormie two up on Curtis Strange and certain to get half a point. So all he needed to do was to get a half himself, while Nelson had to win the hole, to sink his putt and hope that Langer missed his.

Smiling, Langer then asked Nelson if he would take a half for the match, as the two balls "looked good". Surprisingly,

Nelson agreed and it was all over. To make things even better for the European team, a few minutes later the inspirational Seve Ballesteros won his match on the seventeenth, which meant that Europe not just retained the Cup, but had won it again and won it for the first time on American soil. Keeping really alert in matchplay always pays off.

## Lose One, Win One

Gritty determination never to give up, however impossible the situation might look, has also won many matches. You never know at golf. Sometimes an opponent might start to swing the club almost in a state of grace and score far better than he normally does, while suddenly on other holes his ball could bounce wildly off the fairway to end up close behind the only tree in sight, or plug in a grassy bank, or end up on the downslope of a deep bunker. You just never know: all you must do is keep on playing.

Gary Player is probably the most outstanding example of this positive attitude, this competitive drive, whether he was on top of the leader board or far behind in a match. One of the few golfers to win all four majors, he was also supreme at matchplay as he *liked* to beat people, to win. His determination lead him to staging the most famous comeback in the history of the World Matchplay Championship.

Head to head against the gifted American Tony Lema in a 1964 semi-final at Wentworth, Player was six down after the morning round and lost the first hole after lunch – 7 down and 17 to play, a daunting prospect. Surely the match was as good as over. Gary Player certainly didn't think that. He pulled back two holes by the turn and then won the short tenth with a par (a mistake by Lema who missed the green). In fact Lema lost several keyholes to par; the nerves were playing a big part. The crowds were on Player's side, the more they cheered the more uncertain Lema looked. Player gambled with his driver at the eleventh, hitting a huge drive which ended only some 30 yards from the green, setting up a simple pitch and a winning putt for a birdie. He gambled again by taking his driver at the difficult thirteenth and sixteenth holes to win them both in pars. Lema's confidence, by this time, was very ragged indeed and he couldn't control his tee shots. Finally, to square the match, Player risked all again on the eighteenth, hitting his approach close to the trees on the right, drawing it onto the green, close to the flag.

Now Lema was no pushover. He had won the 1964 British Open and was a considerable golfer, with a relaxed, easy manner and a seemingly effortless swing. But on the first play off hole his will to win was more than matched by an inspired, determined Player. Lema's approach hooked into a bunker and shortly after Player sealed a historic win.

If you, as a club golfer, want to win at matchplay you will have to show an equal determination to succeed. Do try to cultivate the same relaxed attitude as Walter Hagan . . . but whatever you do don't give up. You have to keep on playing.

# PRACTICE FOR FUN

There isn't a golfer in the world who doesn't want to play better. To stand on a tee with confidence and hit a gigantic drive, to rifle a long iron to the distant green, to float a high pitch over a deep bunker which pulls up within a foot of the flag: these are the shots that mean you are playing golf, the way you feel sure you should be playing all the time.

But to have this degree of ability requires a lot more hard work than the lazy golfer is able, or willing, to do. He can cut his handicap considerably by concentrating on improving that part of his game that involves judgement and attitude, which is 90 per cent of it. Swinging fluidly and striking the ball better though seems far more important to the vast majority of golfers – and this 10 per cent of the game requires a lot of that dreaded word 'practice'.

Very, very few club golfers really understand what this implies. The practice ground at our fourball's club is almost always deserted. True there is a young lad, a keen beginner, who is sometimes seen at dusk spraying a collection of cut up balls in a wide arc.

Then there is a senior golfer, who potters along every day or so, hitting half a dozen balls lazily, before wandering down to collect them. The local pro also holds his occasional lessons on it . . . but that's about all the action it ever sees.

The members of our fourball have not practised anything for ages. Like 99 per cent of the other club members they have the (unspoken) attitude that anyone who practices is being a bit sneaky and is likely to be, at best, a pothunter. It is just not done, it is not in keeping with the true amateur (Corinthian?) spirit. Which is why Doug occasionally looks furtive when he tells the others he will not be joining them for a week or two as he has to 'work on his game a little'. What he means by this is that he will spend an hour or so at a nearby driving range, blasting two buckets of balls into the blue, in the hope that his acute hook will suddenly, miraculously cure itself. But that is not practice.

Bob, on the other hand, was more or less forced into trying to practice a few years ago when his wife and daughters bought him a practice net as a Christmas present. He suffered much the same galling experiences that Patrick Campbell detailed so amusingly in *Practice Loses the Lot*, having no idea where the shot he was playing was heading. The net now lies mildewing in a corner of his garden shed. And that was not practice either.

## Know Yourself

Golf Clubs in Great Britain, in general, have very poor practice facilities: there is hardly anywhere to practice chipping, pitching or bunker shots. Most of the clubs which do have a practice bunker, should be ashamed of its condition. How on earth are golfers expected to improve when these facilities are so dreadful?

But what is practice? And how should you go about it if you really intend to improve the way you strike the ball? Well, the first thing to realise is that you should not just practice your strengths. This is what most golfers do on a driving range. If they can hit a 3-wood reasonably well, that's the club they use most to work their way through the bucket of balls. True it may lead to more confidence on the tee, but it does not improve the way a golfer strikes his long irons – and that weakness is one he should be practising.

The first essential then is to pinpoint what your weaknesses are. You have to analyse your game, honestly. Now in the US, where they keep statistics on just about everything, they have been busily collecting golfing data for many years. They have charted the performances of top Tour pros to high handicappers and can tell you that, under tournament conditions, the average pro hits ten fairways and nine greens in regulation, taking about 30 putts a round. An 18 handicapper however only manages on average to hit some five fairways and three greens per round and takes about 35 putts.

Knowing how you compare though doesn't really help you with your own game. What you must do is to note how you are playing over three or four weeks. It's quite easy. All you have to do is make a few notes on your card after you've played each hole. You should not be concerned with how many fairways or greens you hit in regulation, nor in the number of mishits you make or penalties you take. What you need to *know* is how well you strike the ball off the tee on average, how solidly you hit your long irons, how competently you play from the sand or chip from the fringe and how well you putt.

So when you're off the green at the end of each hole and the scores are being jotted down, take a note. For each shot you've just played mark down the club used and the way you hit it. If it was a good shot, ending up more or less where you intended, mark a G for good. If it was short, or a bit too bendy, yet ended up just off the fairway, give it an A for average. If it was a mishit, topped, shanked or whatever, put down a B for downright bad.

Marking how you played a par four, say, where you hit a reasonable 3-wood off the tee, a 5-iron that just dropped into a greenside bunker, a sand iron to some 20 feet from the flag and two putts could read: 3wG, 5A, sA, 2p. A par three, where your tee shot ended up on the back fringe, could read: 4A, 7G, 1p. Make sure you note down your performance like this on every hole (unless you have to pick up) for it will surely pay off.

The time for analysis comes when you're back at home and can look at the figures of how you really played with a little concentration. You will not be able to forget that you in fact three putted a few greens, nor that you took a couple each time to get out of several bunkers. But the chances are that your putting isn't *all* that bad and while you need to improve your play from the sand, it may not be the major weakness in your game.

It is much more likely that you will find (especially when you've analysed three or four cards) that, while you are a little wild off the

ANALYSE JUST HOW YOU PLAYED EACH HOLE.

tee, the major fault in your game is your iron play to the green. For this is the case with almost every golfer.

Whatever your weaknesses though, you will at least know them and armed with this information you will have a reason to practice. You can also give yourself a few clear targets to achieve, if you set about it thoughtfully.

## Trials and Try-Outs

Now all Tour pros practice assiduously before and after each tournament round they play. They generally work their way through all the clubs, starting with the 9-iron and ending with the driver, before heading for the putting green. On each course there might be just one shot they need to practice for a particular hole or holes (like a high draw) and they will work on this more than any other.

Generally, if they mishit the ball at all, it will be with the long irons. With often difficult flag placements, there is a need to hit a long iron high into the air and get it to bite into the green. With every course there are also three or four critical shots that have to be hit just right to make all the difference, so these are the ones they practice most. For the rest, mostly 'ordinary' shots, the pros are simply fine-tuning their strike with each club and they believe that the more they get the feel of each, the better they will play the next round.

This is not the case for the club golfer. When you set out for the practice ground, you must only concentrate on improving your weaknesses. But the worst thing to do is to approach any such exercise in a negative frame of mind. You have to believe that it can be very productive to your game and that it can be *fun*, if you choose to make it so.

Your first action when you set your bag down on the ground is to make yourself a 'tee'. Dump your balls down in a heap (no badly cut ones though, please) and lay a club down on the grass, pointing towards a target in the distance, against which you will place your feet. You have to pick the target carefully – and you must know how far away it is, by pacing it out if necessary, or picking another at the right distance for the club you are going to work on.

Without these two basics, any practice is meaningless. Then you can start with a few warm-up shots, but you have to keep in mind just what you are trying to achieve. Are you aiming to hit your 3-iron, say, in a high fade directly at the target? Or hit 20 balls with your 7-iron that end up in a 20-foot circle around it? Whatever your objective for the day, you must stick to it – and don't try to overdo practice. Half-an-hour and 40 balls is a good workout: one hour and 100 balls should be your maximum.

The way the ball flies through the air is the important factor, not how you swing, unless you overbalance. Swinging to a high, elegant follow through counts for nothing, what matters is whether the ball was struck well, towards your target. You have to take your time with each shot and you should, with every one, go through your pre-shot routine (GASP). The more you get into the habit of this discipline, the easier it is to set up and align yourself right when you next play on the course.

Before each shot, you should also try and visualise, to 'see' in your mind's eye, how the ball will fly. Using your imagination like this is a great discipline, recommended by Jack Nicklaus, which helps you to strike the ball well. On the practice ground, to keep yourself motivated and have a little fun, you could also imagine that between you and your target you were faced with a long carry over a lake, or tall trees. When the time comes on the course to play a similar shot 'for real', it will be much less intimidating.

For you have to try and make your practice sessions fun. It is by far the best way to learn a lesson and a little experiment now and then with the club you are working on will keep you fresh throughout a practice workout. If your lack of confidence with your wedge, for example, is a serious chink in your golf armoury, you will have to practice with it. Now consistent length with the wedge is vital and it may be that you have no idea how far the ball will fly. Sometimes it climbs very high and falls well short, or else it bores quite low and finishes way past the flag.

So you have to experiment on the practice ground. The high shots could be because your hands are behind the ball at impact and if this is the case after you've hit a few easy shots, try moving the ball a little back in your stance. If this doesn't work, move it back a touch more until you find *the* ball position that gives you a consistent height and length of shot.

You can also try a similar experiment with your driver, although you probably shouldn't be practising with it unless you're a reasonably good player off the tee with your 3-wood. Let's say straight away that if you are and you still cannot hit your driver, do something about it. Go and talk to your local pro, take his advice, try out other drivers, but *do something about it* at once. Carrying a club in your bag you have little confidence in, especially the driver, is a waste of time. Anyway, assuming you only hit a few very scruffy ones with the club you have, don't just blast away with it at your distant target. Experiment. Try and shape a few shots deliberately right to left. Vary these with high fades. See what happens when you choke down two or three inches on the grip. But every time you are about to hit a shot, think just what it is you are trying to achieve with it.

## Great Games to Score

One of the great things about golf is that you can get an enormous amount of enjoyment pottering about on your own. You can play one ball against another, try equally hard with both and see how you get on. Hit one ball with a driver from the tee, the other with a 3-wood and so on. Some golfers say, 'I can't practice long irons at my course, it's too short'. That's rubbish. All you have to do if you want to practice your three or four irons or even three and five woods, is to take a seven or eight iron off the tee. Imagine, you've got a hole 340 yards long, if you hit 150–160 yards from the tee, you've then got a long shot to the green. A small target, concentrating your mind on the job in hand. On the other hand, if you have a long par four of 460 yards, why not play two 5-irons and then see what you're left with for a third shot. You can ring the changes continuously and there's no excuse to say, because your course is short in yards, you can't play full shots to the green. Use your imagination.

You can also introduce an element of competition into meaningful practice to keep yourself sharp. Once you've achieved, or near enough, your target for the day, you should try and 'wind down' with a few variations, using different clubs. To keep this part of the workout interesting mentally, you can try to compete against yourself in a way that will still help you to learn a few lessons.

One absorbing practice game is to play two balls with each of your clubs, always aiming towards your target. The first ball you should strike with the best of your ability, allowing yourself a Mulligan if you mishit badly. Likewise with the second ball, which you should always try to strike with three quarters of your strength. Wager a mental pint on which strength of shot will consistently give you the most effective results . . . and you may well lose your bet.

Another wind down game is to mentally play two or three holes that you know well on your home course (with or without the three quarter strength swing). Pick a long par four, say, and imagine you're teeing off, so take your drive and aim it at your target. Follow this with your 3-iron and then play your wedge for the last 80 yards (obviously you don't putt out).

You can then pick a par three and hit a smooth 4-iron 'to the green', then follow this with a par five, which needs a driver, 3-wood and an 8-iron. In fact, you could 'play your way round' your course, in your mind, but the complete 18 holes is a little too much for a wind down practice session.

With bunker practice, one of the most important things is to get a club that suits you. Most people play their golf at their home club, unless they're in a team and play away matches or take their clubs on holiday. Bearing that in mind, see what texture of sand you have in the bunkers. If it's very soft and deep you need a club with a big flange; if it's hard and clay like, you will get better results with a thinner soled club. All these things are fairly simplistic and if you ask your professional the right questions, you should get the right answers. If in doubt, ask for a second or even third opinion. Remember when you're trying to get out of a bunker, your stance should be open, the ball opposite the left foot, the back of the club should almost be resting on the sand with the hands forward. The wrists then break quickly and go out, away from the body. You slice under the ball. You have a full swing and a full follow through. You hit under the ball very hard. If your club is swinging at the correct angle, the harder you hit it will only result in the ball going higher. It is basically fear that stops most people from even getting out of a bunker.

Practising in a bunker (if your club has a practice one) is absolutely invaluable. Just playing a series of basic splash shots at the pin is reward enough when it comes to building confidence. But if you want to add a little mental competition, you should try to line up six to ten balls in the bunker, each with a good lie. Splash the first one out towards the flag, but just onto the green.

Then splash the second ball just beyond it, if you can – and keep on trying to make the others each end up a little nearer to the flag each time. It is not as easy as it seems, for you really have to concentrate, but it is a very good game to give you a feel for the distance you splash out. Above all, it gives you a lot of confidence when you next play a round and find yourself in greenside sand.

You can apply the same rules in a similar game with your 7-iron, chipping from the fringe. Rather than just having a few stabs in the general direction of the hole, try and place each ball nearer and nearer it. Or you can try to see how close you get to the hole with three balls, using your 7-iron – and then try another series of three, using your eight. The more variations like this you can inject into your practice sessions, the more interesting they will be and the more ready you will be to play good golf after them.

## Practising on the course

When solitary practice palls, as it will (even though you made yourself do it in the first place) the best remedy is to try a little practice on the course itself. Now let's say right from the start, you must never inconvenience any of your peers. So any such games must be played on days and at the time of day when the course is virtually empty. You have also heard that you should save any tinkering for the practice – and that's true as well. But sometimes you can brighten up your 10 per cent game considerably by trying out a few things on the course and, in this case, preferably with a partner.

Now finding someone to go out with you on a 'practice' round, who will join in the games you intend to try out, is a little like going on a diet. Whenever Brian's wife, for instance, goes on a new diet (which happens about every six weeks or so) she inveigles him to join her on it, despite the fact that he's the last person who needs to lose weight. However, as he never has the option (for she won't cook him anything different from the onion purée or whatever it is she's eating) he stoically has to comply.

You, however, should not have such a problem if you a) seek out a partner who is someone you play with regularly and b) arouse his interest in the type of game you want to play. For you will both benefit from the experience.

For starters, you could play the 'one club challenge'. This was a series on the BBC many years ago, in which two pros and two celebs were each only allowed to choose one club to play nine holes, using it for all their shots. They usually picked a 5-iron, although one or two used a four. If they landed up in the rough or in a bunker, it was all the same. They had to open the club face and play the ball out.

Now this is an absorbing exercise to play against an opponent. For one thing, it teaches you both a great deal about how to use a golf club and about how to play a variety of strokes. For another, it is invariably surprising how well you score with just one club. You may find yourself playing at least to your handicap – and the competition between you will be fun.

Brian, Bob, Doug and Matt played over the last Christmas break in a one club competition. The inspiration of their new club secretary, it was called the *One Club, Fourball, Betterball Challenge.* Starting at 10 am, after a warming drink or two in the clubhouse, two teams of golfers drove off at the same time on every hole on the course to play whatever nine holes lay ahead of them.

Having twisted the secretary's arm, our fourball all played together, Bob (for once) teaming up with Matt and Brian partnering Doug. Matt chose a 4-iron as his one club, with the idea that they needed a degree of length to cope with the demanding par fives. Bob played with a 7-iron, feeling that its left could possibly straighten out his slice (which it did) and that it would make it easier for him to get out of bunkers (which it didn't.)

Brian and Doug both wielded 5-irons and each carried a secret 'weapon': a large hip flask filled with Whisky Mac (to keep out the cold.) These they intended to quaff from on every tee (sharing, of course, with their friendly rivals.) They were confident that even if they did not win the competition, they would win the side-bets, as they had harder heads than either Bob or Matt. They were mistaken.

From the start, on the first hole they played, Bob and Matt were both on the green in three and Bob, striking his ball with the bottom edge of his club, sank the putt for a par. On the next Matt responded with a birdie, having held his club at the bottom of its grip to play a delicate approach which left him with a tap-in. After six holes, their better ball score was level par and they were striding along the fairway, whistling (maybe because of the Whisky Macs) and believing they might just win the Challenge. They had discovered that their choice of club had kept both of them short of real trouble, which is the greatest wrecker of scores, and that while the mechanics

ONE CLUB FUN. DO WE NEED MUCH MORE?

of putting with the edge of the club appeared to be much harder, it seemed to work.

Brian and Doug were faring almost as well, if a little differently. Doug, secure in the knowledge that his long-suffering wife was picking them all up from the club after the competition (so that all could drink festively and not drive) indulged a little too much from his hip flask. After three holes he suddenly developed a serious slice, which so surprised him that he started to chuckle every time be struck the ball, causing Bob and then Matt to accuse him of gamesmanship. Brian however played splendidly. Despite the piercing wind, he strung together a sequence of pars which, coupled with a flukey birdie of Doug's put their better ball score at one over par after six holes played.

All seemed set fair for both teams . . . but then on the seventh Bob and Matt started to find the sand, regularly. With ease, they both notched up a treble bogey, following it with another on their eight. By the time they had both got out of the same greenside bunker on their final hole, their combined better ball score was not much to boast about, although it still seemed quite respectable to them.

Their rivals at first exulted, then slumped. The penultimate hole proved critical. Doug alternated his new-found slice with his usual viscious hook and zig-zagged from rough on the right to rough on the left, finally carding a four over par. Brian matched him, losing one ball (very unusual for him) on his drive – and then losing another over the green.

It made no difference that they both parred the last. "One hole. Just one hole . . . wrecked my best, or possibly best, score . . . ever," said Brian as they ambled merrily towards the clubhouse. Doug chuckled in agreement, wondering if his new slice would be a permanent feature of his game – and one he could count on.

All our heros in the end, regaling themselves in the clubhouse amid general merriment, found themselves very satisfied. Bob and Matt had finished sixth in the order of merit, while Brian and Doug

BRIAN WITH PETER ALLIS, DOUG, BOB AND MATT

were tenth ("But we only *just* didn't win", said Brian.) They all agreed that it had been a really interesting experience, one that they had enjoyed enormously and they all felt that the Whisky Macs had made their swings noticeably more fluid.

Another game to try out, with your full set of clubs, is the one of 'endless Mulligans'. With this game, every time you hit a bad shot you take a Mulligan, play the shot again without penalty. This builds confidence in your swing, as it takes away all the tension of mis-hitting the ball, which wrecks the rounds and fun of so many golfers. You will certainly score much better too and the competition between you and your opponent should be very interesting.

The 'no hazards' practice game will also improve your score, probably by at least 10 shots. In this variation, whenever you get into trouble, be it woods, water, rough or sand, you are allowed to drop the ball out onto the fairway without any penalty. Now while this may not help you to practice your recovery or splash shots, it will help you to swing away with confidence. You will also enjoy the round a lot more when you see how well you've scored, as the chances are your card(s) will be spattered with pars.

Two ball practice games also let you realise what you are capable of playing like, given more expertise in recovery shots. In this variation, you both play two balls for every shot (not the putts) and pick the position of the best one to play the next two shots from. Once again, it helps to build up your confidence on the course, which is what practice is all about. However, if you really want a challenge, you could both try to play your 'worst' ball, which makes you concentrate hard as you have to hit two very good shots from every position.

Play off the tee with a three, five, or even seven iron. This way, you can practice many different second shots to the green on a hole of 320 to 450 yards length. A short course need not hamper your chance to practice long iron or wood approach shots. With such 'games', you could have a lot of pleasure when you need to practice. May you always enjoy the game itself every time you play . . .